C000016479

Medieval Britain

Medieval Britain

Photographs by Andy Williams
Text by Nicholas Best

WEIDENFELD AND NICOLSON
LONDON

INTRODUCTION

$\mathcal{E}$NGLAND has one priceless advantage over most other countries in Europe – it has not had a foreign army on its soil for nearly a thousand years. No enemy troops have rampaged unchecked through its towns and villages, stealing everything they could carry away, burning everything they could not. No generals have waged war on its countryside, ordering the wholesale destruction of anything that might be of comfort to the inhabitants. There have been civil wars, to be sure, and a sustained bombing campaign by the Luftwaffe during the Second World War. But the last civil war was 350 years ago and the damage done by the Germans could have been far worse. By and large, the fabric of the country has suffered far more

from neglect or property development than from the ravages of fire and sword, bomb and bullet.

As a direct consequence, the country still has hundreds, even thousands, of medieval buildings perfectly intact, some of them little changed in 500 years, others much altered in subsequent generations. It has castles, churches, cottages, enormous stately homes and not so enormous manor houses, all sorts and conditions of buildings in all parts of the land. It is perfectly possible for instance to visit York and stand exactly where Richard III did, surrounded by buildings that have hardly altered since his time. Perfectly possible to trace the route taken by Henry II's knights through the cloisters of Canterbury as they went to murder Thomas à Becket, or to look through the same window as Anne Boleyn did when her future husband

Henry VIII swept into the courtyard of Hever Castle for the first time. What follows is a tiny selection of the immense choice on offer. Read the book, then go and see the buildings for yourself!

Eilean Donan Castle

Highlands

*F*ACING the Isle of Skye, Eilean Donan was built in 1220 to repel Viking marauders. It was virtually destroyed in 1719 – when the garrison of Spanish Jacobites was bombarded by an English man-of-war – and restored again after the First World War.

BURY ST EDMUNDS ABBEY

SUFFOLK

*I*N ruins now, Bury St Edmund's abbey was once more than 500 feet long, one of the great churches of England. It marks the grave of King – later Saint – Edmund, murdered by the Danes in 869.

CASTELL COCH

SOUTH GLAMORGAN

COCH is the Welsh for red, and the original castle in Glamorgan was built of red sandstone. It was destroyed in the 15th century, but recreated for the Marquis of Bute in the 1870s.

Tewkesbury Abbey

*T*HE Norman abbey of Tewkesbury was the scene of an extraordinary incident in the Wars of the Roses. Lancastrian leaders defeated at the battle of Tewkesbury fled to the abbey and claimed sanctuary. They were allowed to leave in peace – and then beheaded.

IGHTHAM MOTE

KENT

*T*HE gatehouse at Ightham dates from early Tudor times, although the original house was begun about 1340. It is uncertain whether the house takes its name from the surrounding moat, or from the moot (council meeting) held there in the Middle Ages.

———◆•◆———

URQUHART CASTLE

LOCH NESS

*B*EAUTIFULLY floodlit at night, Urquhart occupies a commanding position over Loch Ness. It features in a famous photograph of the Loch Ness 'monster', taken in 1955 by a Scottish bank manager on holiday with his son.

CHENIES MANOR

BUCKINGHAMSHIRE

*B*UILT by the Cheyne family around 1460, the manor house was later acquired by the Earls of Bedford. In 1542 Henry VIII was staying there with his wife, Catherine Howard, when she committed adultery with Thomas Culpepper.

BAMBURGH CASTLE

NORTHUMBERLAND

*O*verlooking the sea from the top of a 150 foot precipice, Bamburgh traces its origins to a wooden fort built by King Ida in 547. His grandson's wife was called Bebba, from whom the castle's present name derives.

HEVER CASTLE

KENT

*H*EVER is really only a fortified manor house, not a castle at all. It was the childhood home of Anne Boleyn, second wife of Henry VIII. A window in the courtyard is popularly supposed to be the one from which she first saw her future husband.

DOVER CASTLE

KENT

ON a cliff overlooking the harbour, the castle was built soon after the Norman conquest and was still in military use as late as the Second World War. The remains of a Roman lighthouse still stand in the grounds.

———•—•••—•———

EDINBURGH CASTLE

*T*HE walls look formidable enough, but Edinburgh Castle has been captured many times. Robert the Bruce's army took it by a direct assault up the rock face, Sir William Douglas by disguising a dozen Highlanders as merchants and persuading the porter to open the gates.

St Andrew's Cathedral

Fife

*I*N its day, St Andrew's was the largest and most splendid cathedral in Scotland. But the building was attacked by fanatical followers of John Knox and the destruction was completed by Covenanters after the Civil War.

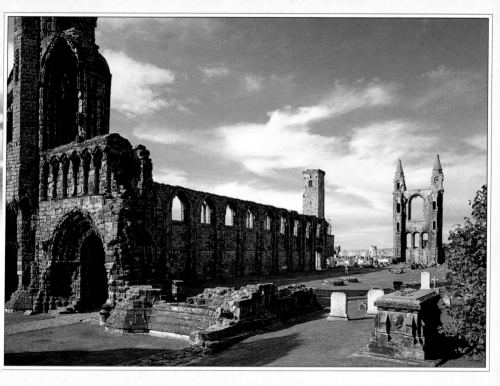

PALACE OF HOLYROODHOUSE

EDINBURGH

HOLYROOD began as a monastery, but later became a royal palace. It was here, on 9 March 1566, that Mary, Queen of Scots, was dining in her private apartments when a group of Scottish noblemen burst in and stabbed her Italian musician, David Riccio, to death.

Glastonbury Abbey

Somerset

According to legend, Joseph of Arimathea built a chapel at the abbey before burying the Holy Grail on Glastonbury Tor nearby. King Arthur and Queen Guinevere are also said to be buried among the ruins.

LEEDS CASTLE

KENT

*A*LTHOUGH it is very old, Leeds has often been rebuilt over the years. Henry VIII spent a fortune turning it from a fort into a palace. The exterior here was largely redesigned again in the 1820s.

WINCHESTER CATHEDRAL

HAMPSHIRE

*T*HERE has been a cathedral at Winchester since Anglo-Saxon times, but the present building was begun in 1079 and completed 300 years later. Jane Austen and King Canute are both buried there.

FOUNTAINS ABBEY

YORKSHIRE

*O*F all the abbeys destroyed by Henry VIII, Fountains is one of the best preserved. Some of its stone was used to build Fountains Hall in 1610, but the rest was protected for future generations by a far-sighted 18th century landowner.

ARUNDEL CASTLE

WEST SUSSEX

*T*HE Duke of Norfolk's ancestors have lived at Arundel for over 700 years. Most of the original castle was destroyed by a parliamentary siege in 1644. The remainder was remodelled in the 19th century.

WEST GATE CANTERBURY

KENT

*T*HE city wall that once protected Canterbury has long since disappeared, but the medieval West Gate remains. By tradition it is the gate by which all reigning monarchs enter the city.

BATTLE ABBEY

SUSSEX

*T*HE abbey was built soon after the Norman conquest, on the edge of the battlefield of Hastings. The great gateway dates from 1338, when the abbot received a licence to crenellate.

TINTERN ABBEY

GWENT

*T*INTERN'S walls have been open to the sky since the 1530s, when Henry VIII dissolved the monasteries and dispersed the monks. Its romantic associations made it very popular with 18th and 19th century tourists, among them William Wordsworth.

LINCOLN CATHEDRAL

LINCOLNSHIRE

*T*HE cathedral was almost completely rebuilt at the end of the 12th century, after an earthquake had destroyed the previous building. Until its spire was blown down in the 16th century, the central tower was the tallest man-made structure in the world.

LINDISFARNE PRIORY

NORTHUMBERLAND

*T*HE Holy Island of
Lindisfarne, just off the
Northumbrian coast, was
an important centre of early
Christianity in England.
The ruins of the priory,
which date from the 11th
century, replaced an earlier
abbey destroyed by the
Vikings.

NEWSTEAD ABBEY

NOTTINGHAMSHIRE

*F*OUNDED in 1170 as a priory for Augustinians, Newstead was given to Sir John Byron after the Dissolution. It was later inherited by Lord Byron, the poet, who alas was too poor to live there.

ACKNOWLEDGEMENTS

Text © Weidenfeld & Nicolson 1995
Photographs © Andy Williams

First published in Great Britain in 1995 by George Weidenfeld & Nicolson Ltd
Orion House, 5 Upper St Martin's Lane, London WC2H 9EA

British Library Cataloguing-in-Publication Data
A catalogue record for this book is available from the British Library

Cover and series design by Peter Bridgewater/Bridgewater Book Company
House Editor: Beth Vaughan

Front cover: Bodiam Castle, East Sussex
Half-title illustration: Corfe Castle, Dorset
Frontispiece: Old Scotney Castle, Kent
Introduction: Warwick Castle, Warwickshire